So Cute! Baby Animals

Puppies

By Katlin Sarantou

Puppies like to play.

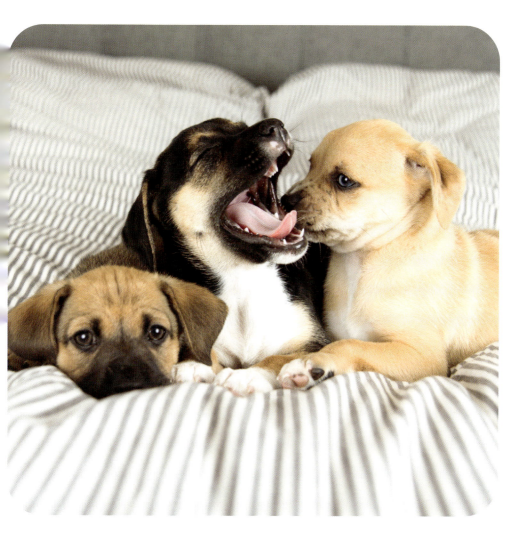

Puppies like to cuddle.

Puppies like to lick.

Puppies like to chase.

Puppies like to sniff.

Puppies like to explore.

Puppies like to fetch.

Puppies like to chew.

Puppies like to stretch.

Puppies like to shake.

Puppies like to splash.

Puppies like to nap.

Word List

Puppies	sniff	shake
play	explore	splash
cuddle	fetch	nap
lick	chew	
chase	stretch	

48 Words

Puppies like to play.
Puppies like to cuddle.
Puppies like to lick.
Puppies like to chase.
Puppies like to sniff.
Puppies like to explore.
Puppies like to fetch.
Puppies like to chew.
Puppies like to stretch.
Puppies like to shake.
Puppies like to splash.
Puppies like to nap.

Published in the United States of America by Cherry Lake Publishing Group
Ann Arbor, Michigan
www.cherrylakepublishing.com

Photo Credits: © Ivanova N/Shutterstock.com, cover, 1; © Sundays Photography/Shutterstock.com, 2; © Anna Hoychuk/Shutterstock.com, 3; © Sergey Lavrentev/Shutterstock.com, 4; © Orientgold/Shutterstock.com, 5; © Tony Kan/Shutterstock.com, 6; © Jackie Neff/Shutterstock.com, 7; © Life In Pixels/Shutterstock.com, 8; © Asiya Yunussova/Shutterstock.com, 9; © Ivanova N/Shutterstock.com, 10; © ANURAK PONGPATIMET/Shutterstock.com, 11, 13; © Grigorita Ko/Shutterstock.com, 12; © Scorpp/Shutterstock.com, 14, back cover

Copyright © 2021 by Cherry Lake Publishing Group
All rights reserved. No part of this book may be reproduced or utilized in any form or by any means without written permission from the publisher.

Cherry Blossom Press is an imprint of Cherry Lake Publishing Group.

Library of Congress Cataloging-in-Publication Data

Names: Sarantou, Katlin, author.
Title: Puppies / by Katlin Sarantou.
Description: Ann Arbor, Michigan : Cherry Lake Publishing, [2021] | Series: So cute! baby animals | Audience: Grades K-1 | Summary: "Aww. How cute! Early readers will learn about what puppies like to do. The simple text makes it easy for children to engage in reading. Books use the Whole Language approach to literacy, a combination of sight words and repetition that builds recognition and confidence. Bold, colorful photographs correlate directly to the text to help guide readers through the book"— Provided by publisher.
Identifiers: LCCN 2020032072 (print) | LCCN 2020032073 (ebook) | ISBN 9781534179875 (paperback) | ISBN 9781534180888 (pdf) | ISBN 9781534182592 (ebook)
Subjects: LCSH: Puppies—Juvenile literature.
Classification: LCC SF426.5 .S27 2021 (print) | LCC SF426.5 (ebook) | DDC 636.7/07—dc23
LC record available at https://lccn.loc.gov/2020032072
LC ebook record available at https://lccn.loc.gov/2020032073

Printed in the United States of America
Corporate Graphics